easy BLUE flute duets

James Rae

www.universaledition.com
vienna · london · new york

UE 21 320
ISMN M-008-07721-0
UPC 8-03452-06085-7
ISBN 3-7024-3008-3

Preface

These duets for elementary level players are written within a comfortable range and will serve as an introduction to the various blues styles. Both parts are of an equal technical level. The pieces are fun to play in music lessons and would make excellent performance items for school concerts and music festivals.

A Note about Swing Quavers

In a lot of Jazz music, the quavers are often said to be swung. This means that the first of every pair of quavers on the beat is twice as long as the second (tripletised). Sometimes they are written as straight quavers ♫ and sometimes as a dotted quaver followed by a semi-quaver ♩., but there will always be an indication of the style from the tempo marking, e.g. Swing feel. Many composers now use the symbol ♫ = ♩♪ to denote that all quavers in the music should be swung.

N.B. This also applies to quaver rests.

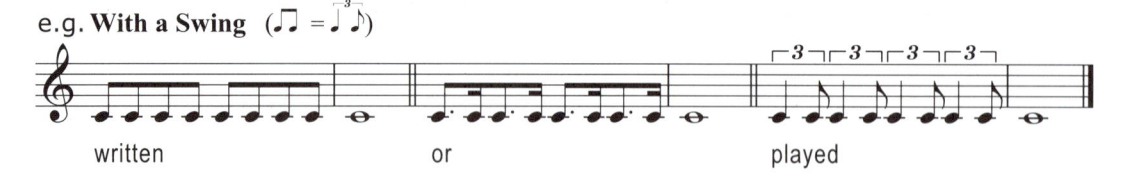

e.g. **With a Swing** (♫ = ♩♪)

written   or   played

Vorwort

Diese Duette sind in einer für Spieler der Elementarstufe angenehmen Lage geschrieben und dienen als Einführung für verschiedene Stilarten des Blues. Beide Stimmen haben das gleiche technische Niveau. Die Stücke eignen sich gut für den Instrumentalunterricht und können auch hervorragend bei Schulkonzerten und Musikfestivals eingesetzt werden.

Hinweise zu swingend gespielten Achtelnoten

Im Jazz sollen die Achtelnoten häufig *swingend* gespielt werden. Das heißt, dass die erste von zwei Achtelnoten pro Zählzeit doppelt so lang ist wie die zweite (triolisch). Manchmal werden sie wie *normale* Achtelnoten ♫ und manchmal punktiert ♩. notiert, aber es gibt immer eine Anmerkung des Stils bei der Tempobezeichnung, z. B. *Swing feel*. Viele Komponisten verwenden heutzutage auch das Symbol ♫ = ♩♪, um darauf hinzuweisen, dass alle Achtelnoten in der Musik swingend gespielt werden sollen.

Übrigens: Das trifft auch auf Achtelpausen zu.

z.B. **With a Swing** (♫ = ♩♪)

notiert   oder   gespielt

Préface

Ces duos d'un niveau élémentaire, écrits dans une tessiture confortable, représentent une introduction aux différents styles de blues. Les deux parties sont d'un même niveau technique. Agréables à jouer pendant les cours, ils seront aussi d'excellentes pièces pour les auditions de l'école et autres concerts.

Indications pour les croches devant dans le style swing

Dans de nombreuses musiques de jazz, les croches sont souvent qualifiées d'« oscillantes » : ceci signifie que la première de chaque paire sur le temps est deux fois plus longue que la seconde (triplée). Quelquefois elles sont écrites comme des noires « régulières » ♪♪ et quelquefois comme croche pointée/doubles croches ♪♪. Mais il y aura toujours une indication du style à partir de l'indication de tempo, par example *Swing feel*. Aujourd'hui de nombreux compositeurs utilisent le symbole ♪♪ = ♪♪ pour signifier que toutes les croches de la musique devraient être oscillantes.

N.B. Ceci s'applique aussi aux demi soupirs.

p.ex. **With a Swing** (♪♪ = ♪♪)

écrit   ou   joué

Contents • Inhalt • Table des Matières

Watch Out!	6
Waltzin' with the Blues	7
Blue Reflections	8
Blue Magic	9
Igneous Rock	10
Pendulum Blues	11
Cutting it Fine	12
Message Deleted!	13
Mr Awkward	14
Funky Download	15

Watch Out!

James Rae

Waltzin' with the Blues

James Rae

Blue Reflections

James Rae

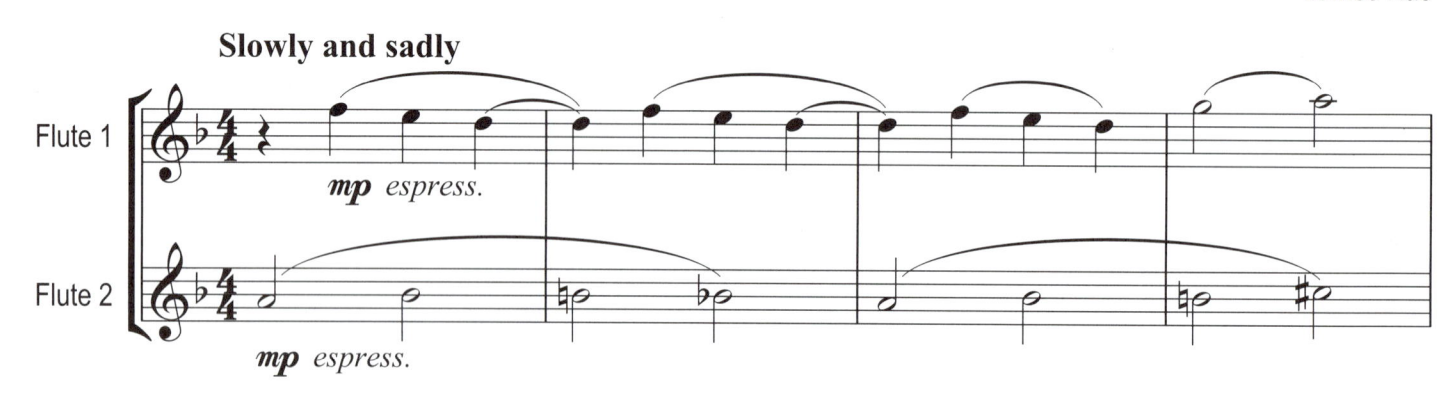

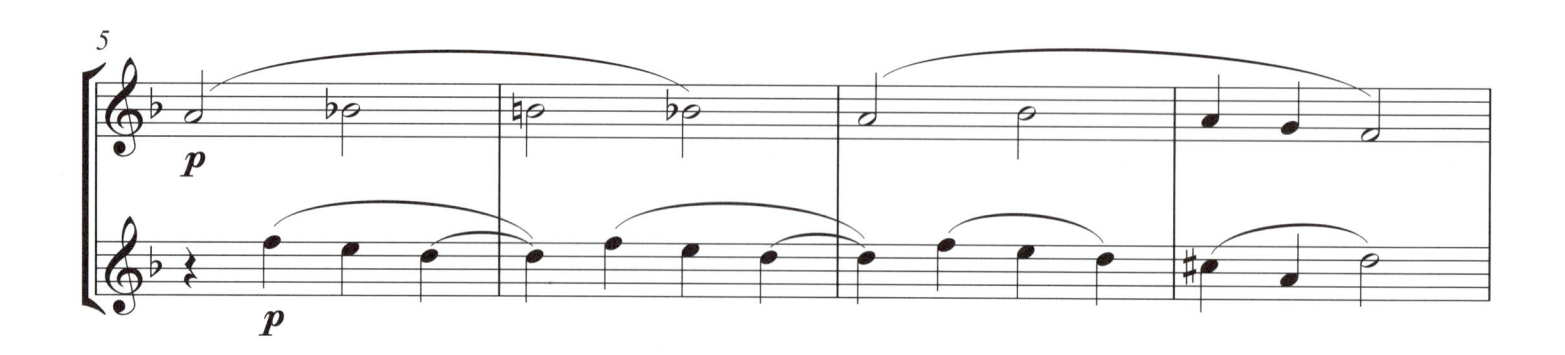

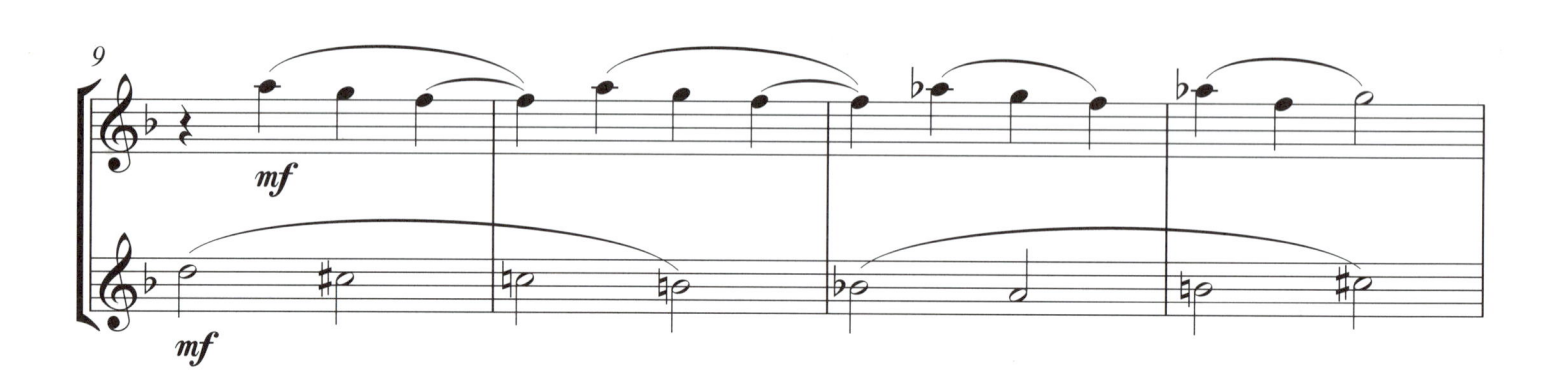

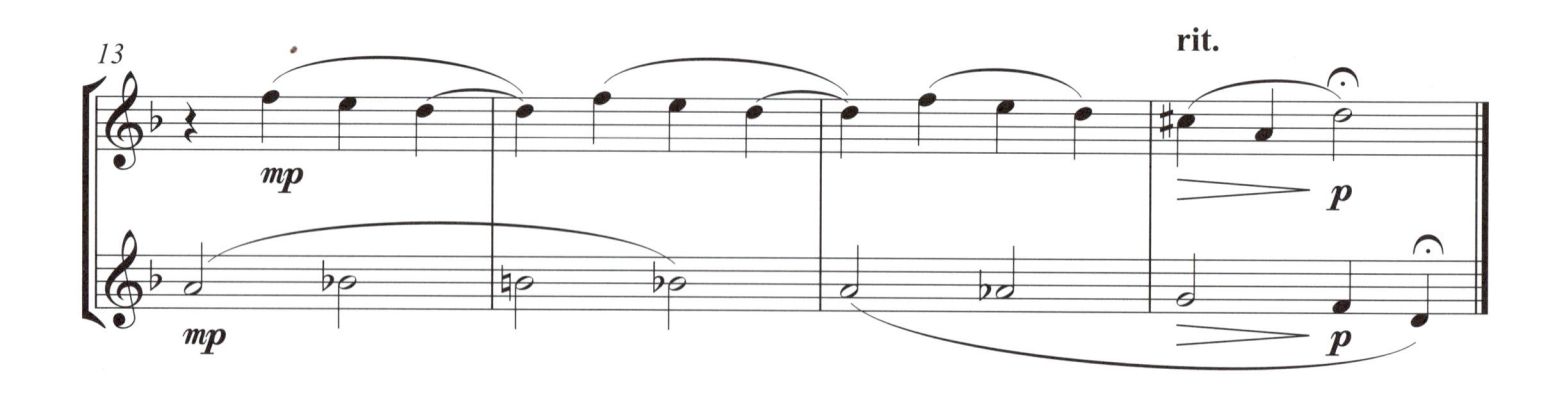

Blue Magic

James Rae

Igneous Rock

James Rae

Pendulum Blues

James Rae

Cutting it Fine

James Rae

Message Deleted!

James Rae

Mr Awkward

James Rae

Funky Download

James Rae

James Rae
Style Workout – Flute

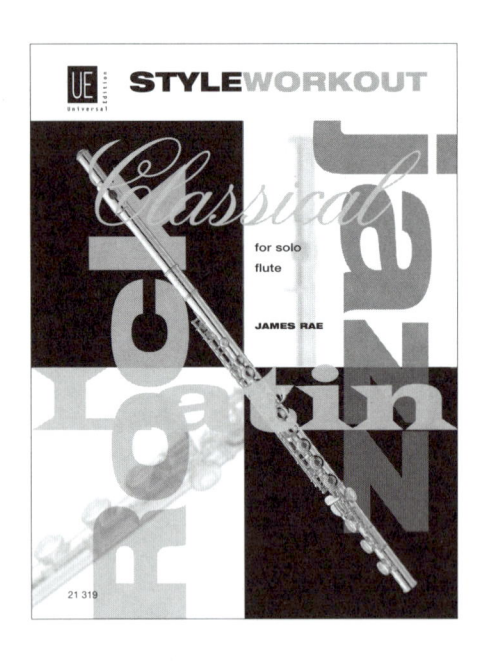

James Rae
Style Workout – Flute
40 studies in classical, jazz, rock and latin styles

easy – intermediate level
UE 21319
ISMN M-008-07720-3

This book will provide players from grade 1 to intermediate level with their own style 'workouts'. 40 original studies are grouped together in four sections – Classical, Jazz, Rock and Latin – all in player-friendly keys to maximize concentration on STYLE.

James Rae includes hints and tips with each piece and a Listening List to support his strong advice that listening to all types of music is essential for acquiring a 'feel' for musical style. Inspiring and fun workouts.

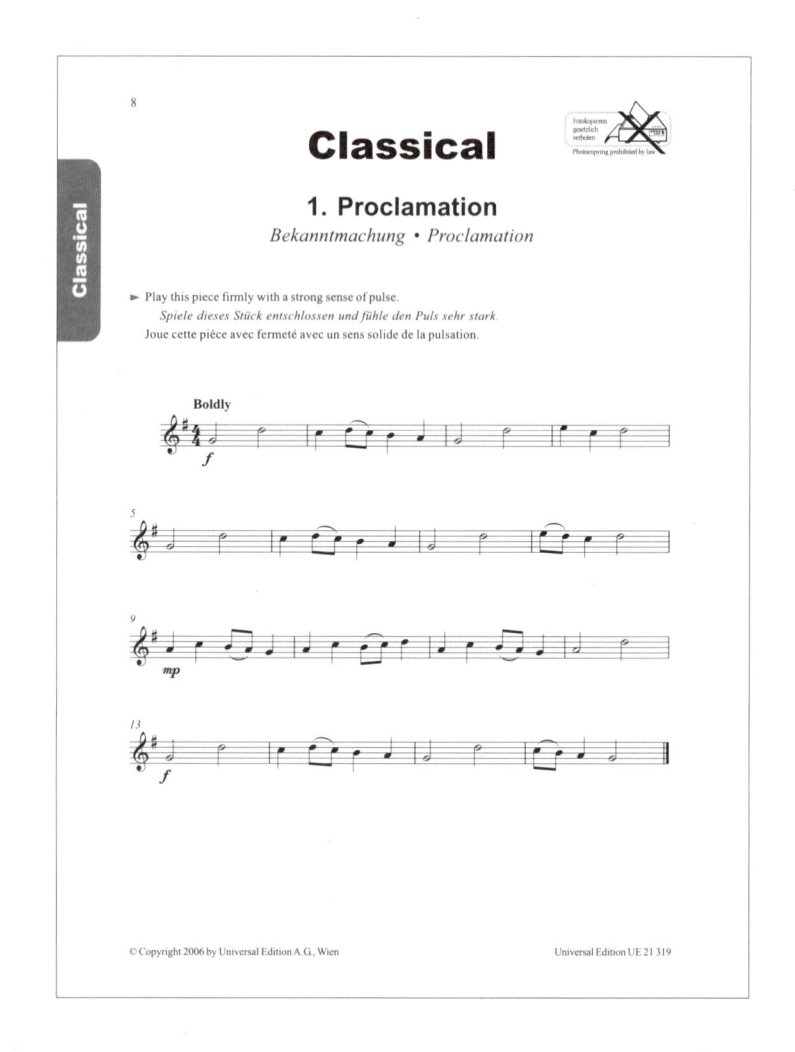

Diese 40 Originalkompositionen geben von Klassik über Jazz und Rock bis hin zu Latin die gesamte Bandbreite musikalischer Vielfalt wider. Jedes Stück stellt einen typischen Aspekt des jeweiligen Stils in den Vordergrund. Hierbei helfen kurze und einprägsame Tipps bei der Umsetzung und unterstützen den jungen Musiker sinnvoll.

Darüber hinaus gibt die sogenannte „Listening List" mit Vorschlägen von Mozart bis Stan Getz Anregungen zum hörenden Erfassen des Feelings.